Preface

This farewell book is a tribute to remember the special memories and thoughts shared between friends, colleagues, staff, and instructors.

This farewell book serves as a repository for storing heartfelt messages of gratitude, meaningful guidance, cherished photos, and memories from time spent together in educational institutions like schools, colleges, universities, and other organizations.

It serves as a reminder of the lasting impact these relationships have had on your lives and a celebration of the friendships formed.

Although you may be bidding farewell to your academic institution, the memories will endure forever.

ipCreativeWorks
we foresee

THIS BOOK BELONGS TO

My Recollections

My Recollections.... :

____

____

____

____

____

____

____

____

____

____

____

____

____

____

____

____

____

____

Institution:

Education:

Duration of study from _____________ *to* _____________

Name: ______________________________

📞 ______________________ ✉ ______________________

Personal Reflection

____

____

____

____

____

Favorite Memories

____

____

____

____

____

A Message of Appreciation

____

____

____

____

____

Advisory & Final Message to me

____

____

____

____

____

____

Name: _______________________________

📞 _____________________ ✉ _____________________

Personal Reflection

____

____

____

____

____

Favorite Memories

____

____

____

____

____

A Message of Appreciation

____

____

____

____

____

Advisory & Final Message to me

____

____

____

____

____

____

Name: ____

📞 _____________________   ✉ _____________________

Personal Reflection

____
____
____
____
____

Favorite Memories

____
____
____
____
____

A Message of Appreciation

____
____
____
____
____

Advisory & Final Message to me

____
____
____
____
____
____

Name: _______________________________

☎ _______________________ ✉ _______________________

Personal Reflection

____

____

____

____

____

Favorite Memories

____

____

____

____

____

A Message of Appreciation

____

____

____

____

____

Advisory & Final Message to me

____

____

____

____

____

____

Name: _______________________

📞 _________________ ✉ _____________________

Personal Reflection

____
____
____
____
____

Favorite Memories

____
____
____
____
____

A Message of Appreciation

____
____
____
____

Advisory & Final Message to me

____
____
____
____
____
____

Name: ______________________________

☎ ____________________ ✉ ______________________

Personal Reflection

____
____
____
____
____

Favorite Memories

____
____
____
____
____

A Message of Appreciation

____
____
____
____
____

Advisory & Final Message to me

____
____
____
____
____
____

Name: ___________________________

📞 ___________________ ✉ ___________________

Personal Reflection

____

____

____

____

____

Favorite Memories

____

____

____

____

____

A Message of Appreciation

____

____

____

____

____

Advisory & Final Message to me

____

____

____

____

____

____

Name: _______________________________

📞 ____________________ ✉ _______________________

Personal Reflection

____
____
____
____
____

Favorite Memories

____
____
____
____
____

A Message of Appreciation

____
____
____
____

Advisory & Final Message to me

____
____
____
____
____

Name: _______________________

☎ _____________________ ✉ _________________________

Personal Reflection

____

____

____

____

____

Favorite Memories

____

____

____

____

____

A Message of Appreciation

____

____

____

____

____

Advisory & Final Message to me

____

____

____

____

____

____

Name: _______________________________

📞 _______________________ ✉ _______________________

Personal Reflection

____

____

____

____

Favorite Memories

____

____

____

____

A Message of Appreciation

____

____

____

____

Advisory & Final Message to me

____

____

____

____

____

Name: _______________________________

☎ _____________________ ✉ _______________________

Personal Reflection

____

____

____

____

____

Favorite Memories

____

____

____

____

____

A Message of Appreciation

____

____

____

____

____

Advisory & Final Message to me

____

____

____

____

____

____

Name: _______________________________

📞 _____________________ ✉ _____________________

Personal Reflection

____

____

____

____

Favorite Memories

____

____

____

____

A Message of Appreciation

____

____

____

____

Advisory & Final Message to me

____

____

____

____

____

____

Name: _______________________________

☎ _________________________ ✉ _________________________

Personal Reflection

____

____

____

____

____

Favorite Memories

____

____

____

____

____

A Message of Appreciation

____

____

____

____

____

Advisory & Final Message to me

____

____

____

____

____

____

Name: _______________________________

📞 _____________________ ✉ _____________________________

Personal Reflection

____

____

____

____

Favorite Memories

____

____

____

____

A Message of Appreciation

____

____

____

____

Advisory & Final Message to me

____

____

____

____

____

Name: _______________________________

📞 _____________________ ✉ _______________________

Personal Reflection

____

____

____

____

Favorite Memories

____

____

____

____

A Message of Appreciation

____

____

____

____

Advisory & Final Message to me

____

____

____

____

____

Name: ____

📞 _________________________ ✉ _______________________________

Personal Reflection

____

____

____

____

____

Favorite Memories

____

____

____

____

____

A Message of Appreciation

____

____

____

____

____

Advisory & Final Message to me

____

____

____

____

____

____

Name: __________________________________

☎ ____________________ ✉ ____________________

Personal Reflection

____

____

____

____

Favorite Memories

____

____

____

____

A Message of Appreciation

____

____

____

____

Advisory & Final Message to me

____

____

____

____

____

____

Name: ________________________________

📞 ____________________ ✉ ____________________

Personal Reflection

____

____

____

____

____

Favorite Memories

____

____

____

____

____

A Message of Appreciation

____

____

____

____

____

Advisory & Final Message to me

____

____

____

____

____

____

Name: _______________________________

📞 _____________________   ✉ _______________________

Personal Reflection

____

____

____

____

Favorite Memories

____

____

____

____

A Message of Appreciation

____

____

____

____

Advisory & Final Message to me

____

____

____

____

____

____

Name: ________________________________

☎ ________________________ ✉ ________________________________

Personal Reflection

____

____

____

____

____

Favorite Memories

____

____

____

____

____

A Message of Appreciation

____

____

____

____

____

Advisory & Final Message to me

____

____

____

____

____

____

Name: _______________________________

📞 _______________________ ✉ _______________________

Personal Reflection

Favorite Memories

A Message of Appreciation

Advisory & Final Message to me

Name: ____________________________

📞 __________________ ✉ __________________

Personal Reflection

____

____

____

____

____

Favorite Memories

____

____

____

____

____

A Message of Appreciation

____

____

____

____

____

Advisory & Final Message to me

____

____

____

____

____

____

____

Name: _______________________________

📞 _____________________ ✉ _______________________

Personal Reflection

____

____

____

____

____

Favorite Memories

____

____

____

____

____

A Message of Appreciation

____

____

____

____

____

Advisory & Final Message to me

____

____

____

____

____

____

Name: ___________________________

📞 _________________________   ✉ _________________________

Personal Reflection

____

____

____

____

Favorite Memories

____

____

____

____

A Message of Appreciation

____

____

____

____

Advisory & Final Message to me

____

____

____

____

____

Name: ___________________________

📞 ___________________ ✉ ___________________

Personal Reflection

Favorite Memories

A Message of Appreciation

Advisory & Final Message to me

Name: _______________________________

📞 _______________ ✉ _______________________

Personal Reflection

____

____

____

____

____

Favorite Memories

____

____

____

____

A Message of Appreciation

____

____

____

____

Advisory & Final Message to me

____

____

____

____

____

Name: ___________________________________

☎ ___________________ ✉ ___________________________

Personal Reflection

____

____

____

____

____

Favorite Memories

____

____

____

____

____

A Message of Appreciation

____

____

____

____

Advisory & Final Message to me

____

____

____

____

____

Name: _______________________________

☎ ___________________ ✉ ___________________

Personal Reflection

____
____
____
____
____

Favorite Memories

____
____
____
____
____

A Message of Appreciation

____
____
____
____
____

Advisory & Final Message to me

____
____
____
____
____
____

Name: ____________________________________

📞 __________________ ✉ ________________________

Personal Reflection

____

____

____

____

____

Favorite Memories

____

____

____

____

____

A Message of Appreciation

____

____

____

____

____

Advisory & Final Message to me

____

____

____

____

____

Name: _______________________________

📞 ________________ ✉ ________________________

Personal Reflection

____

____

____

____

____

Favorite Memories

____

____

____

____

____

A Message of Appreciation

____

____

____

____

Advisory & Final Message to me

____

____

____

____

____

____

Name: _______________________________

📞 _______________________ ✉ _______________________

Personal Reflection

____

____

____

____

____

Favorite Memories

____

____

____

____

____

A Message of Appreciation

____

____

____

____

Advisory & Final Message to me

____

____

____

____

____

____

Name: _______________________________

☎ _______________________ ✉ _______________________

Personal Reflection

____
____
____
____
____

Favorite Memories

____
____
____
____
____

A Message of Appreciation

____
____
____
____
____

Advisory & Final Message to me

____
____
____
____
____
____

Name: _______________________________

📞 _______________________   ✉ _______________________

Personal Reflection

____

____

____

____

____

Favorite Memories

____

____

____

____

____

A Message of Appreciation

____

____

____

____

Advisory & Final Message to me

____

____

____

____

____

____

Name: _______________________________

📞 _________________   ✉ _______________________

Personal Reflection

____

____

____

____

____

Favorite Memories

____

____

____

____

____

A Message of Appreciation

____

____

____

____

____

Advisory & Final Message to me

____

____

____

____

____

Name: _______________________

📞 _____________________ ✉ _______________________

Personal Reflection

____

____

____

____

Favorite Memories

____

____

____

____

A Message of Appreciation

____

____

____

____

Advisory & Final Message to me

____

____

____

____

Name: _______________________________

📞 ___________________ ✉ ___________________

Personal Reflection

____
____
____
____

Favorite Memories

____
____
____
____

A Message of Appreciation

____
____
____
____

Advisory & Final Message to me

____
____
____
____
____
____

Name: _______________________________

☎ _________________________ ✉ _________________________

Personal Reflection

____

____

____

____

____

Favorite Memories

____

____

____

____

____

A Message of Appreciation

____

____

____

____

____

Advisory & Final Message to me

____

____

____

____

____

____

Name: _______________________________

📞 _________________________ ✉ _________________________

Personal Reflection

____

____

____

____

____

Favorite Memories

____

____

____

____

A Message of Appreciation

____

____

____

____

Advisory & Final Message to me

____

____

____

____

____

____

Name: ____

☎ ___________________ ✉ _________________________

Personal Reflection

____

____

____

____

Favorite Memories

____

____

____

____

A Message of Appreciation

____

____

____

____

Advisory & Final Message to me

____

____

____

____

____

____

Name: ______________________________

📞 _____________________   ✉ ______________________

Personal Reflection

____

____

____

____

____

Favorite Memories

____

____

____

____

____

A Message of Appreciation

____

____

____

____

____

Advisory & Final Message to me

____

____

____

____

____

Name: _______________________________

📞 _____________________ ✉ _____________________

Personal Reflection

____

____

____

____

Favorite Memories

____

____

____

____

A Message of Appreciation

____

____

____

____

Advisory & Final Message to me

____

____

____

____

____

____

Name: _______________________________

☎ _____________________ ✉ _______________________

Personal Reflection

____

____

____

____

____

Favorite Memories

____

____

____

____

____

A Message of Appreciation

____

____

____

____

____

Advisory & Final Message to me

____

____

____

____

____

____

Name: _______________________

📞 _____________________ ✉ _____________________

Personal Reflection

Favorite Memories

A Message of Appreciation

Advisory & Final Message to me

Name: _______________________________

📞 ________________ ✉ _________________________

Personal Reflection

____
____
____
____
____

Favorite Memories

____
____
____
____
____

A Message of Appreciation

____
____
____
____
____

Advisory & Final Message to me

____
____
____
____
____
____

Name: _______________________________

📞 _______________________ ✉ ______________________________

Personal Reflection

____
____
____
____

Favorite Memories

____
____
____
____

A Message of Appreciation

____
____
____
____

Advisory & Final Message to me

____
____
____
____
____
____

Name: ________________________

☎ ________________________   ✉ ________________________

Personal Reflection

____

____

____

____

Favorite Memories

____

____

____

____

A Message of Appreciation

____

____

____

____

Advisory & Final Message to me

____

____

____

____

Name: ____

☎ _____________________ ✉ _________________________

Personal Reflection

____
____
____
____
____

Favorite Memories

____
____
____
____

A Message of Appreciation

____
____
____
____

Advisory & Final Message to me

____
____
____
____
____
____

Name: ____

☎ ___________________ ✉ ___________________________

Personal Reflection

____
____
____
____

Favorite Memories

____
____
____
____

A Message of Appreciation

____
____
____
____

Advisory & Final Message to me

____
____
____
____
____

Name: _______________________

📞 _______________ ✉ _______________

Personal Reflection

____
____
____
____

Favorite Memories

____
____
____
____

A Message of Appreciation

____
____
____
____

Advisory & Final Message to me

____
____
____
____
____

Name: _______________________________

📞 _______________________ ✉ _______________________

Personal Reflection

____

____

____

____

____

Favorite Memories

____

____

____

____

____

A Message of Appreciation

____

____

____

____

____

Advisory & Final Message to me

____

____

____

____

____

____

Friendship Quotations

1. "One best book is equal to a hundred good friends, but one good friend is equal to a library" - **APJ Abdul Kalam**
2. "A true friend is someone who is always there during the good times and the bad times." - **Oprah Winfrey**
3. "A friend is someone who gives you total freedom to be yourself." - **Jim Morrison**
4. "A friend is someone who knows all about you and still loves you." - **Elbert Hubbard**
5. "Friendship is the only cement that will ever hold the world together." - **Woodrow T. Wilson**
6. "Old friends are gold, and new friends are diamonds. If you get diamonds don't forget gold because the only gold can hold diamonds." - **APJ Abdul Kalam**
7. "The most beautiful discovery true friends make is that they can grow separately without growing apart." - **Elizabeth Foley**
8. "The only way to have a good friend is to be one." - **Ralph Waldo Emerson**
9. "Friendship is a single soul dwelling in two bodies." - **Aristotle**.
10. "Making a hundred friends is not a miracle; the miracle is to make one friend who will standby your side even if hundreds are against you" - **APJ Abdul Kalam**

Dear Friends

THANK YOU.